The Teens' Solution Workbook

by Lawrence E. Shapiro, Ph.D.

The Center for Applied Psychology, Inc.
King of Prussia, Pennsylvania

The Teens' Solution Workbook
by Lawrence E. Shapiro, Ph.D.

Published by:
The Center for Applied Psychology, Inc.
P.O. Box 61587, King of Prussia, PA 19406 U.S.A.
Telephone: 1-800-962-1141

The Center for Applied Psychology, Inc. is the publisher of Childswork/Childsplay, a catalog of products for mental health professionals, teachers, and parents who wish to help children with their social and emotional growth.

Printed in the United States of America.

ISBN 1-882732-62-6

TABLE OF CONTENTS

Principles of Solution-Oriented Therapy

INTRODUCTION

Over the last five years, Solution-Oriented Therapy has become an increasingly popular approach to dealing with a wide variety of problems. Solution-oriented thinking is very different from problem-oriented thinking. It looks at the positive, rather than the negative. It looks at the present and the future, rather than the past. It looks at the ways that you can make your life better, rather than the things that have made it bad.

Simplicity is one of the basic tenets of this approach. Solution-oriented thinking avoids jargon and "psychobabble." It relies on common sense. Solution-oriented thinking assumes that you are smart, not dumb, even though you may be bewildered and "stuck" regarding a particular problem you are having. It assumes that you have already solved many problems in your life, and in fact you probably have a warehouse full of solutions that have already worked for you. The idea behind this workbook is to help you use solutions that you have already found, and to use them on the problems that presently bother you.

This workbook consists of activities based on the principles of Solution-Oriented Therapy. There is no wrong way to do any of these activities. You can start at the beginning and go through the book, or start anywhere else that you like. Maybe one activity will be enough. Maybe you will want to do them all. The important thing to remember is to stop dwelling on your problems and look for new ways to enjoy and enrich your life.

EXERCISE #1:
BEGIN BY ADOPTING A
SOLUTION-ORIENTED ATTITUDE

If you are like most teens, you probably feel like you have many problems...and you're probably right. A problem could be something that frustrates you, something that makes you feel upset, something that causes difficulty for others, or simply two incompatible ideas. Life is full of problems for all of us, but teens do seem to have more problems than either children or adults, because they are caught between these two different worlds with very different expectations.

But that doesn't mean that you can't learn to solve your problems, or at least to cope with them better. When you learn to cope with a problem, you are aware of it, but you don't let it affect other areas of your life. For example, imagine two people, each one of whom has hurt his/her knee in an accident.

Person A:

- Stays in bed for a week until he can walk without pain.
- Stops talking to his friends until he feels better because they get on his nerves.
- Sneaks a drink when his parents are away because it helps with the pain.
- Doesn't bother doing any schoolwork because his knee bothers him too much to concentrate.

Person B:

- Gets crutches so that she can continue her life as normally as possible.
- Takes aspirin for the pain.
- Finds a gym with a whirlpool, because the doctor said it might heal the muscle quicker.
- Keeps up with her friends and her schoolwork because it takes her mind off her physical problem.

As you can see, the problem is the same for Persons A and B, but each copes with it differently. Person A probably creates even more problems for himself. Person B minimizes the effect of the problem. These same principles apply to psychological problems and interpersonal problems as well. The way you choose to cope with them is entirely up to you.

PROBLEM LIST

Name: _____ Date: _____

A. Start by making a list of all your problems, big and small. Don't hold back. List as many as you like, no matter how small they may seem.

1. _____

2. _____

3. _____

4. _____

5. _____

6. _____

7. _____

8. _____

9. _____

10. _____

11. _____

12. _____

13. _____

14. _____

15. _____

16. _____

17. _____

18. _____

19. _____

20. _____

TOP 10 PROBLEMS

B. Now go back and choose the top 10 problems and write them below.

1. _____
2. _____
3. _____
4. _____
5. _____
6. _____
7. _____
8. _____
9. _____
10. _____

10 LEAST IMPORTANT PROBLEMS

C. Now go back and choose the 10 least important problems and write them below.

1. _____
2. _____
3. _____
4. _____
5. _____
6. _____
7. _____
8. _____
9. _____
10. _____

D. Now look at your lists from Exercises B and C, and write the three problems with which you already have found ways to cope. Do you cope better with easier problems or harder problems? Some people are surprised to learn that they actually cope better with harder problems and they let the easy ones really bother them. Write down five ways in which you already cope with these problems.

Name: _____ Date: _____

Problem #1:

_____
_____
_____
_____
_____

Five Ways in Which You Already Cope:

1. _____
2. _____
3. _____
4. _____
5. _____

Problem #2:

_____
_____
_____
_____
_____

Five Ways in Which You Already Cope:

1. _____
2. _____
3. _____
4. _____
5. _____

Problem #3:

_____
_____
_____
_____
_____

Five Ways in Which You Already Cope:

1. _____
2. _____
3. _____
4. _____
5. _____

EXERCISE #2:
SIMPLER IS BETTER

Although some people feel that you should start with the hardest or most serious problem first, this really doesn't make sense from a psychological point of view. If you were learning to drive for the first time, you would naturally start by learning the basics, probably just driving around an empty parking lot. You wouldn't start by driving through a major city, trying to race from one end to the other as quickly as you could.

A basic principle of solution-oriented thinking is to start with simple problems first—problems that you can solve easily.

A. List 10 problems that you currently have. Then rank them from 1 to 10, with 1 being the hardest to solve and 10 being the easiest.

Name: _____	Date: _____
Problems	**Rank**

B. Now pick the easiest of your top 10 problems to solve. Write about it below in as much detail as possible.

_____

_____

_____

_____

_____

_____

_____

_____

_____

_____

_____

_____

_____

_____

_____

_____

C. This exercise is designed to "lubricate" your solution-oriented thinking. In learning to brainstorm new solutions, you must come up with as many ideas as possible, without worrying about whether they are good or bad, practical or impractical, smart or dumb. Just come up with new ideas.

To get you started practicing brainstorming, I want you to think of new ways to use a trash can. Imagine an ordinary, metal, medium-size trash can like you might find in an office or a classroom. Now think of all the things you can use the trash can for other than for depositing trash. *Don't worry about whether they are good ideas or not; just write!*

EXERCISE #3:
WHEN YOU'RE STUCK ON A PROBLEM, "BRAINSTORM" SOLUTIONS

In developing a solution-oriented style of thinking, it is important to stop thinking about why solutions won't work and to concentrate on why they will.

One of the main differences between people who are overwhelmed by their problems and those who are not is that the solution-oriented people have trained themselves to see solutions in places where others don't even bother to look.

Finding solutions to your problems requires that you change your style of thinking. It's not that hard, it just requires a little practice. Unless, of course, you are so much in love with your problems that you'd just as soon hang on to them...

BRAINSTORM SOLUTIONS

A. Did you come up with 10 ideas or more? If you didn't, you might consider getting a friend or two to help you brainstorm. Some people seem to be better at generating ideas than others, but nearly everyone gets more ideas when someone else is helping. Try a similar "practice" exercise with a friend. This time, take a book, a nickel and a ruler. Think of as many ways as you can to use at least two of these objects together, and you get bonus points if you can use all three at the same time.

Name: _____ Date: _____

1. _____
2. _____
3. _____
4. _____
5. _____
6. _____
7. _____
8. _____
9. _____
10. _____
11. _____
12. _____
13. _____
14. _____
15. _____
16. _____
17. _____
18. _____
19. _____
20. _____

B. Having fun yet? If not, your next exercise is to think of how generating ideas can be more fun.

This is very basic psychology: People will practice what they enjoy doing and will avoid what is difficult. So if you do not enjoy brainstorming, you probably won't do it, and you're going to have more difficulty in finding solutions than many other people.

One way to make a difficult task more enjoyable is to pair it with something you already enjoy. That's why people listen to music while they work or munch on popcorn while they study.

If you had to solve a problem right now, how could you make generating solutions to that problem more enjoyable? Write as many things as you can think of below. Don't worry if they are good ideas or bad ones. Just write!

Name: _____ Date: _____

I can make generating solutions to my problem more enjoyable by. . .

1. _____

2. _____

3. _____

4. _____

5. _____

6. _____

7. _____

8. _____

9. _____

10. _____

C. Now it's time to take the next step in evaluating ideas. Go back to the previous exercise and select only the ideas that are feasible and realistic. Write them below.

Ways to Help Me Brainstorm Solutions

1. _____
2. _____
3. _____
4. _____
5. _____
6. _____
7. _____
8. _____
9. _____
10. _____

EXERCISE #4:
USE SOLUTION-ORIENTED LANGUAGE

One of the most important ways to start changing problems into solutions is to start talking about new possibilities and directions. Some of the worst things you can do is to put labels on people or look for and dwell on negative things. *When you communicate in solution-oriented language, you will be more likely to see solutions to the problem.*

A. For the first *exercise* in using solution-oriented language, *see* if you can stop labeling or stereotyping other people. Here are common "labels" that you may use when you are angry or frustrated:

stupid
idiot
retard
dictator
creep

Actually, you probably use much more colorful language than this, but I don't want to put those words in print.

The point is that while labeling someone who is part of a problem you are having feels good for the moment because it releases your anger, it doesn't help you solve the problem. In fact, it makes things worse. Labeling of any type keeps you from seeing possible solutions.

Try thinking of people in terms of behaviors that you don't like, rather than just labeling them. For example, if your father grounded you for a month because you were one hour late for a curfew, rather than thinking of him as a "dictator," you could think, "I don't like the way he punishes me without even a discussion." A possible solution to this problem then becomes clearer: Find a way to agree on specific and reasonable punishments when specific rules are broken.

Try this exercise in changing negative labels that you might use in talking about people who cause you problems. Instead of using a label, describe the behavior that you don't like.

Name: _____ Date: _____

AVOIDING LABELS

Label/Stereotype	Describe Behavior

B. Another problem people often have in solving problems is thinking and talking in "absolute" terms. Words like "always," "never," and "everyone" are considered to be absolutes because they don't allow for the possibility of even one exception. Absolutes shut the door on finding new ways to approach a problem.

Below, write some statements that you currently use which are absolutes. Then try and think of better ways to say them which are more specific. Finally, think of whether this new way to describe a problem opens up a possibility of a solution and write about it.

Example:

Absolute Statement

My mom is always nagging me about how I look.

More Specific Statement

My mom gives me a disapproving look when I wear my torn-up jeans to school.

Possible Solutions

Don't wear the jeans to school.
Tell Mom that her look irritates me and ask her not to do it.
Have a conversation about my rights as a teenager with Mom.

Name: _____   Date: _____

Step #1: Absolute Statement	Step #2: More Specific Statement	Step #3: Possible Solutions
Step #1: Absolute Statement	Step #2: More Specific Statement	Step #3: Possible Solutions
Step #1: Absolute Statement	Step #2: More Specific Statement	Step #3: Possible Solutions
Step #1: Absolute Statement	Step #2: More Specific Statement	Step #3: Possible Solutions

C. When you begin to stop thinking in terms of "absolute" statements, you will probably notice how much other people use them. To find new solutions to your problems, you may have to teach other people to stop talking in absolutes as well. Listen for when other people talk in absolutes. Write them down before you mention them to the other person. Try to understand for yourself the specific thing they are trying to say.

Write some examples below:

Name: _____ Date: _____	
Absolute Statement (Made by _____)	More Specific Statement
_____	_____
_____	_____
_____	_____
_____	_____
Absolute Statement (Made by _____)	More Specific Statement
_____	_____
_____	_____
_____	_____
_____	_____
Absolute Statement (Made by _____)	More Specific Statement
_____	_____
_____	_____
_____	_____
_____	_____
Absolute Statement (Made by _____)	More Specific Statement
_____	_____
_____	_____
_____	_____
_____	_____

D. Correcting the way other people think can be a tricky issue. When someone makes a statement as an "absolute," it becomes untrue, and yet calling someone a "liar" will surely not contribute to finding a solution to a problem. Usually the other person is using an "absolute" statement to express a feeling, and that feeling distorts the reality of the statement.

Try restating another person's absolute statement as a more specific one and state the feeling behind the absolute statement as well. For example, suppose you are late coming home for dinner and your mother says:

"You are always late. Can't you ever be on time?"

You could say:

"I know you are angry that I am late for dinner tonight. I'm sorry."

This will not solve the problem. Your mother might still be angry and might punish you. But it might help open up a solution-oriented conversation.

Try to think of some absolute statements that people make to you and write a restatement of what they are saying, noting the feeling and the specifics behind their statements.

Name: _____	Date: _____

Absolute Statement (Made by _____)	Restatement (include feeling, specifics)
_____	_____
_____	_____
_____	_____
_____	_____
_____	_____

Absolute Statement (Made by _____)	Restatement (include feeling, specifics)
_____	_____
_____	_____
_____	_____
_____	_____
_____	_____

Absolute Statement (Made by _____)	Restatement (include feeling, specifics)
_____	_____
_____	_____
_____	_____
_____	_____
_____	_____

Absolute Statement (Made by _____)	Restatement (include feeling, specifics)
_____	_____
_____	_____
_____	_____
_____	_____
_____	_____

E. It isn't easy to change the way you think and talk. But it can make a tremendous difference in your life, and particularly in the nature of your problems.

Diplomats, negotiators, and other "peacemakers" have learned the art of using language to solve problems.

Try this exercise in seeing another person's point of view by looking at that person's negative or critical statement as his or her "need." Remember that seeing another person's point of view doesn't mean that you have to agree with it, but rather that you recognize it.

Let's look at the example from the previous exercise. Your mother says:

"You're always late. Can't you ever be on time?"

Now write down what she needs and why she needs it.

She needs to have everyone at the table on time so she doesn't have
   to worry about reheating the dinner.
She needs to have her family together.
She needs order and predictability in her life to make it less
   stressful.

Remember, you don't have to agree with any of this. This exercise is just about seeing something from another person's point of view.

Now write some critical statements that people have made to you recently, and try to figure out what they need and what they were trying to express.

Name: _____ Date: _____

Negative Statement (Made by _____)	What needs were behind the statement?
_____	_____
_____	_____
_____	_____
_____	_____
_____	_____
_____	_____

Negative Statement (Made by _____)	What needs were behind the statement?
_____	_____
_____	_____
_____	_____
_____	_____
_____	_____
_____	_____

Negative Statement (Made by _____)	What needs were behind the statement?
_____	_____
_____	_____
_____	_____
_____	_____
_____	_____
_____	_____

Negative Statement (Made by _____)	What needs were behind the statement?
_____	_____
_____	_____
_____	_____
_____	_____
_____	_____

EXERCISE #5:
USE A "SOLUTION" TO SOLVE MORE THAN ONE PROBLEM AT A TIME

Once you start thinking in terms of solutions rather than problems, you will start to see how one solution can relate to more than one problem. For example, suppose your parents are criticizing you about your grades, your study habits, and how much time you talk on the phone. Each of these problems is related to time and how you spend it. Now suppose you can negotiate a contract with your parents stating that you will spend a designated amount of time in required activities such as homework and chores, and if you accomplish this, they will be more lenient about your phone time. One solution solves three problems.

A. List five problems you are having. Then look for one thing they have in common. Can you think of one change you could make or negotiate which could influence two or more problems at the same time?

Name: _____ Date: _____

Problems

_____

_____

_____

_____

Write down what they have in common:

_____

_____

_____

_____

Write down a possible common solution:

_____

_____

_____

_____

B. A central idea behind solution-oriented thinking is that problems are related, and solving one small problem will effect other positive changes. It is like throwing a pebble in a pond: There is a ripple effect which spreads out from the center in all directions.

Imagine that when you take the first step to solving a problem it spreads out and affects many other people and situations. Write the first change that you will make in the center circle, and then write in the people or situations that might be affected (even in a small way) by your change in the next circle.

Step #1:
People/Situations Affected:

Step #2:
People/Situations Affected:

Step #3:
People/Situations Affected:

Step #4:
People/Situations Affected:

Step #5:
People/Situations Affected:

C. Problems tend to isolate people. It seems to be in our human nature (or at least in our culture) to think that we must bear a problem alone or that no one else has had this problem before. Obviously, neither of these thoughts is true.

Think of three people you know who have found solutions for problems similar to the ones you have now. Write their names below and the problem as you understand it. Then call them on the phone and ask them what they did. Be open and candid. Write anything that might help you with your current concern.

Be a little unconventional when looking for solutions. They may not be obvious. *Remember that people find solutions to very serious problems every day! You can, too.*

1. Person: _____

His/Her Problem: _____

_____

What You Learned: _____

_____

2. Person: _____

His/Her Problem: _____

_____

What You Learned: _____

_____

3. Person: _____

His/Her Problem: _____

_____

What You Learned: _____

_____

D. As mentioned in the previous exercise, people tend to isolate themselves with their problems, and this tends to make the problem worse. Learn to rely on other people to help you with a problem you are having. Remember, you are not in this alone.

Write the names of 10 people who can help, even in a very small way. Don't be shy about asking for help. Wouldn't you do the same for someone else?

1. Person: _____

_____

The Way He/She Can Help: _____

_____

_____

When He/She Can Help: _____

_____

_____

2. Person: _____

_____

The Way He/She Can Help: _____

_____

_____

When He/She Can Help: _____

_____

_____

3. Person: _____

_____

The Way He/She Can Help: _____

_____

_____

When He/She Can Help: _____

_____

_____

4. Person: _____

_____

The Way He/She Can Help: _____

_____

_____

When He/She Can Help: _____

_____

_____

E. Many cultures stress the role of family and community in solving problems. But for many reasons, this seems to be the exception rather than the rule for most Americans. However, you can create a network to help you with a problem. A network could include friends, family, a self-help group, people whom you have met "on-line," and so on.

On the next page, list 10 people whom you could consider as your "network." These are the people who would always be there for you if you needed them. Also list each person's most obvious strength in supporting you or helping you with a problem. For example, some people are good listeners, and others are very action-oriented. One person might be very good at helping you solve concrete problems (like finding a part-time job), and someone else might be good at helping you with more abstract problems (like how to survive a teacher you can't stand). Write down the strength of each person in your network at helping you find solutions to your problems.

Name: _____   Date: _____

Person	His/Her Strength in Solving Problems
1.	
2.	
3.	
4.	
5.	
6.	
7.	
8.	
9.	
10.	

EXERCISE #6:
FIND SOLUTIONS IN SMALL STEPS

Problems are best solved in small steps. When you think in small steps, even problems that seem to be insurmountable can be solved.

Think of a goal for yourself. Now write 20 small steps to get to that goal. When you make the steps or subgoals very small, they are much easier to attain.

Child's Name: _____ Date: _____

Goal: _____

Subgoals	Criteria for Success
Step #1 _____	_____
Step #2 _____	_____
Step #3 _____	_____
Step #4 _____	_____
Step #5 _____	_____
Step #6 _____	_____
Step #7 _____	_____
Step #8 _____	_____
Step #9 _____	_____
Step #10 _____	_____

Subgoals	Criteria for Success
Step #11 _____	_____
Step #12 _____	_____
Step #13 _____	_____
Step #14 _____	_____
Step #15 _____	_____
Step #16 _____	_____
Step #17 _____	_____
Step #18 _____	_____
Step #19 _____	_____
Step #20 _____	_____

EXERCISE #7:
ANTICIPATE SUCCESS

Psychologists have long recognized the ability people have to unconsciously create their future. Without thinking about it, they put themselves in situations or make decisions based on needs or conflicts of which they are not really aware. Some people define "neurotic behavior" as behavior that makes things worse for themselves or for others even though this is not their desire. But our minds can also unconsciously work to make our lives better.

Recognizing the importance of our unconscious wishes and needs, Solution-Oriented Therapy asks people to concentrate on how things will be in a future where the problem has less influence or may be absent altogether. Concentrating on the positive aspects of our lives, rather than on the problems, directs our unconscious to make decisions that will be more productive and beneficial. The concept of a "self-fulfilling prophecy" is a very real psychological phenomenon. You can make your future better or worse—why not make it better?

A. Imagine that the problem that now confounds you is gone in six months or a year. Write about how your life has changed for the better. Be very specific. Be positive, but also be realistic.

Name: _____ Date: _____

_____

_____

_____

_____

_____

_____

_____

_____

_____

_____

_____

_____

B. Now reread what you wrote in the previous paragraph. Does anything come to mind that will make this scene happen? Even if it isn't directly related to the problem, write it down. Tear out this exercise (or make a copy of it) and read it frequently, perhaps once a week. Keep reading about the future. Convince yourself that it can happen. Keep thinking about even the simplest of ways to make positive changes in your life.

Things to Do Differently to Make Positive Changes in My Life:

1. _____
2. _____
3. _____
4. _____
5. _____
6. _____
7. _____
8. _____
9. _____
10. _____
11. _____
12. _____
13. _____
14. _____
15. _____

EXERCISE #8:
THINK ABOUT YOUR PROBLEMS WITH "REALISTIC OPTIMISM"

Having a positive attitude really does make a difference. Studies have shown optimistic people are less likely to be depressed, perform better at work, and are even physically healthier. Being optimistic is more than just an attitude—it is a way of explaining the world. Optimists see the world realistically. They see bad events as single occurrences, rather than bad luck or fate. They believe that over time, problems work themselves out. They also take responsibility for their actions, knowing when to hold themselves accountable for decisions and when other people are in control of events.

Pessimists distort the way they think. They overgeneralize (e.g., "I always have the worst luck"), they personalize events (e.g., "Everyone is against me"), and they exaggerate negative occurrences (e.g., "This is the worst day of my life!").

Many studies have demonstrated that people can learn to change their pessimistic thinking into more optimistic thinking.

A. Write about a pessimistic way of looking at the worst day you had this month.

_____

_____

_____

_____

_____

_____

_____

_____

_____

_____

_____

_____

B. Now write about the same event from the viewpoint of an optimist. Don't be unrealistic. Just be positive in seeing bad things as single events which can changed and good things as events which can be perpetuated.

_____

_____

_____

_____

_____

_____

_____

_____

_____

_____

_____

_____

EXERCISE #9:
LEARN FROM FAILURE

Most people avoid failure at any cost. They think that if people perceive them as a failure, they will think there is something very wrong with them.

These people don't understand that there are two types of failures: one that results from not trying and one that comes from trying but not getting the right answer. There is no excuse if you fail from not trying. That might be your decision, but it is rarely a good one. Failure as a process of trying is another matter altogether. Persistent effort in the face of failure is a mark of character and frequently leads to successes that you might not have ever imagined.

Consider how many great discoveries were the result of failures. Thomas Edison failed hundreds of times before he was able to discover the components for the electric lightbulb. Paul Ehrlich, who discovered a drug that would cure syphilis in the early part of this century, also failed hundreds of times before he discovered the correct formula. In fact, the name for his final formula was 606, since the prior 605 experiments were failures.

A. Can you think of a time when you didn't succeed, but you learned something anyway? If it didn't happen to you, maybe it happened to someone you know.

_____

_____

_____

_____

_____

_____

_____

_____

_____

_____

_____

_____

B. Can you think of something you did where you couldn't imagine being stopped by failure? Maybe it was learning to play the guitar or learning to drive a car.

Write what happened the first time you failed at this and what you did immediately afterwards.

_____

_____

_____

_____

_____

_____

_____

_____

_____

_____

_____

EXERCISE #10:
"SHAPE" SOLUTIONS BY POSITIVELY
REINFORCING PEOPLE'S BEHAVIOR

Behavioral shaping is a type of behavior modification to which we are all susceptible. And it really works!

If people keep telling us we look good when wearing clothes of a certain color, we will start to wear more of that color, without even really being aware that our habits are changing.

The same principle holds true for the people in your life. If you praise someone for doing something you like, he or she will tend to do it again. Other types of positive reinforcement are conveyed through body language and just showing an interest in what someone is saying. You can't get someone to do something that he really doesn't want to do using this technique, but you can "shape" his behavior in a direction in which he might go anyway.

A. How might you shape the behavior of someone who can help you find a solution to a problem you are currently having?

First, define the problem you are having:

_____

_____

Now, write the person's name and what you would like that person to do more (Note: He or she must do the behavior at least occasionally in order for you to reinforce it):

Person's Name: _____

I want him/her to: _____

_____

Now write how you might reinforce that behavior and when:

Type of Behavior That Occurs From Person	Type of Reinforcement to Shape Behavior
_____	_____
_____	_____
_____	_____
_____	_____
_____	_____
_____	_____

B. Try shaping a person's behavior for one week. Write down each time the behavior occurs and see if it becomes more frequent.

Person's Name:		
Person's Behavior:		

Date	Time	How You Reinforced It

EXERCISE #11:
USE SOLUTION-ORIENTED COPING SKILLS

It would be naive to think that your problems will change unless you change as well. People get "stuck" in the way that they look at their problems, and you must find ways to get "unstuck." This does not necessarily mean that you will have to make radical changes. An important assumption of solution-oriented thinking is that even small changes can make a big difference.

Check the things you could do differently in order to take a different approach to a problem.

_____ Talk to an adult and get advice.

_____ Take a deep breath and relax instead of getting stressed or losing your cool.

_____ Take a more positive attitude.

_____ Get help from a friend.

_____ Find a new behavior which can act as a substitute for the problem.

_____ Read a book about the problem.

_____ Find someone who has had a similar problem and talk about it.

_____ Stick up for your rights.

_____ Other _____

EXERCISE #12:
TAKE CONTROL OF YOUR PROBLEMS

Some people let problems control their lives. Every decision they make and everything they do is related to the problem.

But this doesn't have to be the case. Many people have very serious problems, yet they manage to put them into a small corner of their lives. They just decide that the problem will not control them and that they will be in control.

A. For one week, keep a record of who is in control of your life—your problem or you. Mark it on a 10-point scale with:

1 = *The problem is in control*
10 = *I'm in control*

See if you find yourself more in control each day. Why are some days better than others? What can you do to stay in complete control over your own life?

The Problem
Is in Control   I'm in Control

Monday | 1 | | 2 | | 3 | | 4 | | 5 | | 6 | | 7 | | 8 | | 9 | | 10 |

Comments: _____

_____

Tuesday | 1 | | 2 | | 3 | | 4 | | 5 | | 6 | | 7 | | 8 | | 9 | | 10 |

Comments: _____

_____

Wednesday | 1 | | 2 | | 3 | | 4 | | 5 | | 6 | | 7 | | 8 | | 9 | | 10 |

Comments: _____

_____

Thursday | 1 | | 2 | | 3 | | 4 | | 5 | | 6 | | 7 | | 8 | | 9 | | 10 |

Comments: _____

_____

The Problem
Is in Control   I'm in Control

Friday | 1 | | 2 | | 3 | | 4 | | 5 | | 6 | | 7 | | 8 | | 9 | | 10 |

Comments: _____

_____

Saturday | 1 | | 2 | | 3 | | 4 | | 5 | | 6 | | 7 | | 8 | | 9 | | 10 |

Comments: _____

_____

Sunday | 1 | | 2 | | 3 | | 4 | | 5 | | 6 | | 7 | | 8 | | 9 | | 10 |

Comments: _____

_____

B. Many people get stuck on problems and don't bother trying to find solutions. This often has to do with the way they think about their problems. Changing a problem into a "goal" is a much more positive way to think and will show you a direction in which you can change.

For example, Ned was always getting picked on at school because he was short. Just a few kids started it, but then it seemed like everyone who saw him had something insulting to say. He made a simple goal for himself: "I'm going to find one person who is intelligent enough to like me as I am and considerate enough not to tease me." He found that one person in his computer class and spent more time with him, ignoring the teasing of the other kids.

Can you change your "problem" into a "goal"? Maybe answering these questions will help.

What is something you can work towards that will make you happy?

_____

_____

What is the opposite of your problem?

_____

_____

What is an activity that will help you forget your problem?

_____

_____

What is something that you can do, every day, that will help you with your problem?

_____

_____

What is a goal that you could work towards that would make your problem go away, or at least seem less important?

_____

_____

EXERCISE #13:
CONCENTRATE ON THE PRESENT AND THE FUTURE RATHER THAN ON THE PAST

Some people say that every day is like a new page in the book of your life. You can write whatever you like! If you want, you can write today's page as a continuation of your problems, or you can start fresh! Suppose that today your story didn't have the same problems as you had yesterday or the day before. Suppose that today you began writing your problem out of your life!

How would you begin to write your problem out of your life? What will today (or tomorrow) look like if your problem does not play such an important part?

Try writing about just one day in your life that is a fresh start. Write about a day that doesn't have your problem in it, or at least not very much. Can you make it happen?

Name: _____ Date: _____

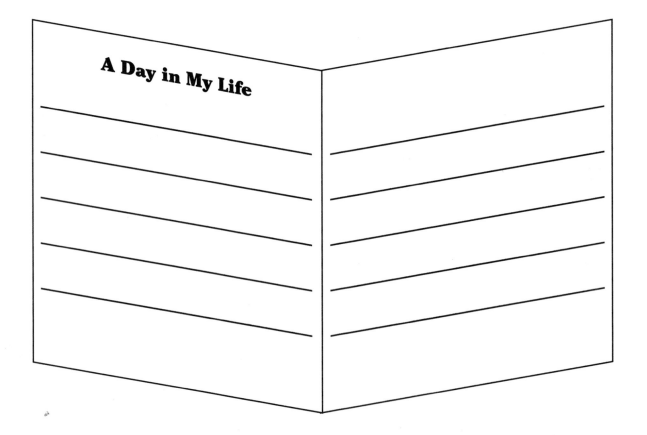

A Day in My Life

EXERCISE #14:
FOCUS ON THE POSSIBLE AND CHANGEABLE

Sometimes change is easy, and at other times it is difficult. For example, smoking is a difficult habit to change because cigarettes have a drug in them (nicotine) which is addictive. That's why adults are always telling kids not to start smoking, because it is so hard to stop. Other things are easy to change. Wanda's parents were concerned that everyone in the family watched too much TV. So they just put their TV in the closet and only took it out for one hour a night.

When you think about changing a problem that you have, you will see that there are many things that you could do and many places to start. But some ways to start are easier, and some are harder.

Write five things that you could change right away to help solve a problem you are having. Then circle the one that is really easy. Then do it!

Name: _____ Date: _____

Define the Problem: _____

_____

Things I Can Change Right Away to Help Solve My Problem

1. _____

2. _____

3. _____

4. _____

5. _____

EXERCISE #15:
UNDERSTAND THAT CHANGE IS CONSTANT

Everything changes all of the time. Whatever problem you have today will be different tomorrow, even though it might be different in just a small way.

Think about how things will change for the problem that you are concerned about. Will change make things easier? If not, why not, and what can you do about it?

How will your problem change one month from now?

_____

_____

Six months from now?

_____

_____

One year from now?

_____

_____

Two years from now?

_____

_____

Five years from now?

_____

_____

EXERCISE #16:
CHANGE THE THINGS THAT KEEP SOLUTIONS FROM OCCURRING

Have you ever tried to solve a problem but felt that everything was working against you? Maybe you were right. Maybe there were so many forces keeping the problem going that you just couldn't change it. Kate, for example, had a serious weight problem. She tried to diet, but her parents served fattening foods at every meal. For dinner, they might have fried chicken and mashed potatoes and gravy, all of which Kate loved. Even when Kate used all her willpower and asked for something less fattening to eat, her mom just got mad and said, "This is what I cooked for dinner. Eat this or go hungry." So Kate ate what the rest of her family ate so that her mother wouldn't be mad.

What about the problem you are having? Is there anyone who is keeping the problem from getting better even though he or she doesn't intend to? Be careful before you blame other people for your problems. You must take responsibility for change. But you can also ask for help and point out to others that their behavior affects your problems.

Make a list of the people you know well and write one thing that each person could do to make a problem easier for you to solve. Then ask them if they will do it. If they won't, don't be upset. You simply need to find other people who can help you.

Name: _____

Date: _____

WHO ELSE CAN CHANGE TO HELP YOU FIND A SOLUTION?

Person	How He/She Can Change	Check (3) if He/She Agrees to Change

REFERENCES

Cade, B. and O'Hanlon, W. H. *A Brief Guide to Brief Therapy*. New York/London: W.W. Norton & Company (1993).

de Shazer, S. *Keys to Solutions in Brief Therapy*. New York/London: W.W. Norton & Company (1984).

Epston, D. and White M. *Narrative Means to Therapeutic Ends*. New York/London: W.W. Norton & Company (1990).

Haley, J. *Problem-Solving Therapy*. New York: Harper & Row (1976).

Metcalf, L. *Counseling Toward Solutions*. West Nyack: The Center for Applied Research Education (1995).

O'Hanlon, W. H. and Weiner-Davis, M. *In Search of Solutions: A New Direction in Psychotherapy*. New York/London: W.W. Norton & Company (1989).